Acknowledgements

There have been so many wonderful people over the years that have provided me with solace and support; My wife Shelley is always there for me; and my daughters Amber and Willow contribute greatly to this soul; I have a son I rarely see but is always in my thoughts; The gang at the Onyx and at the old Moondog were instrumental to my poetic well-being, I salute each one of you especially, Ben, Milo, Nate, Chris, Richard, Mike, Katie, Donn, Jack, Consuelo, Linda and especially Brandon for all his hard work. We have had some most poetic times.

UNPROTECTED POETRY

LARRY JAFFE

Photography by Felix Kunze
ISBN-13: 978-1492853299
ISBN-10: 1492853291

Introduction

Many years ago I wrote a poem called Unprotected Poetry. Little did I know at the time that this not so simple, not so little poem would create such controversy. For over ten years Unprotected Poetry has assaulted the senses of readers and listeners all looking to see or hear between the lines. That this most sensual poem could be about censorship was not always understood but the concept was readily appreciated.

Thank you for your help and support and may all your poetry be unprotected.

Larry Jaffe

ONE-EYED SPLENDOR

I see you with one eye because
my other eye is too busy confronting reality.
With my right eye I take in your grace and beauty
while my other eye is jaundiced
by the man on the corner in rags
begging for food or drink and maybe work.

Then I see your smile working hard
to get my attention
but when I watch the news
about some drive by shooting
of children my attention is split
and now I have one eye crying
and the other smiling back at you

My life feels crossed as my eyes peel away
in opposite directions.
One eye wants to enjoy life
and the other crying because of it.

It splits me apart right down the middle
and it is not that I don't love you
I just don't know how to love life
when it looks at me this way.

I always keep one eye peeled for trouble
and the other aimed for pleasure.
You see, life has me coming and going
I look both ways when I cross the street
but I cannot wait for the light to change
to make my moves.

cannot wait for permission mother may I
to breathe my life.
My fingers fly across my keyboard
creating beauty in people's lives

so undernourished by pain.
My one eye feeling the blemish
my other trying to be optimistic.

but I am having trouble
because I paid the wrong dues
and now my membership is up.
And when I see you lying
there in erotic slumber
I want to close my bad eye.

I want to close my bad eye
when I walk down the street
even if it is Beverly Hills
because behind that façade
of rich and famous
lies this empty rice bowl soul.

And I want to close my bad eye
because it cries so damn much
and on that side I am running out of tears
tears of submission tears of admission
tears of seduction tears of reduction
too many damn tears bleeding
from that damn eye.
While the other stays awake
doing crossword puzzles
and writing love songs
and perhaps dripping
a tear of joy now and then.

But things are way out of balance
my tear ducts are out of balance
my emotions no longer harmonious
I see shadows playing in darkness
and I wonder
if my good eye
has any tears to spare.

FIVE AND DIME STORE DREAMS

I grew up with Woolworths
and Kresges
five & dime stores
cause everything
was supposed to be
on the cheap
growing up
I did not understand
where the buffalo roam
we just sang songs about it
we were Woody Guthrie
without his guitar
traveling through music
to find our highways
we were taught
to cover our heads
in bomb scare drills
way before terrorism was born
we fought the commie treasure
fear of being nuked
fallout shelters the rage
and then we raged
through 60's hoopla
warring factions of peace
but my heart resided
in that 5 & dime
where peace was affordable

STEEL-TOED BUTTERFLY

They called her steel-toed butterfly
because her steel-toed working woman's boots
protected her person from ravaged dreams
and devastated illusion

Her feet firmly planted
finding their way home
ankles no longer chained
by shackles of a fictitious love

She wore wings of carved pathos
and shocked arousal
woven through threads of
blood red raw silk gown

This steel toed butterfly
breathed air inhaled from heaven
she was butterfly
not angel

Wings cloaked
her countenance
hiding the pain
and discomfort
of earthly tribute
donations
she unwittingly made

And now her face a façade
of unrequited intellect
and only the drunken passion
she never desired was returned

Her steel-toed beauty
defied description
almost prehistoric

radiating from soulful source
features moderated by demeanor
the soul the window to her heart

Sheathed in her smile
was the happiness she once sought
the mountains she climbed
in personal triumph
were headlines
in yesterday's
news magazines

She was a steel-toed butterfly
yanking boot straps
to help her fly
she appeared
like the miracle
of morning dew
the gently cupped hands
that tried to capture her
were the invisible
shackles of past love

CAN'T GO IN THERE

You can't go in there
the sign said
colored only
no whites allowed

You can't go in there son
the gas station attendant
rubbed me the wrong way
with his gaze and words
and attitude

You can't go in there boy
the one you want is over
there he pointed with
drool and grease
encrusted finger

I looked up at him
with new man's eyes
of teenage assertion
knowing I had just
became a man
in god's eyes
freshly Bar Mitzvahed

You can't go in there boy
the sign said
colored only
no whites allowed
I just need to pee
I muttered
under my breath

I just need to pee
and really did not care
what the damn sign said
never having seen
such scenic revulsion before
living in my savant
suburban cocoon
all these years

You can't go in there boy
I am not a boy
I am a man now
I can go anywhere I want
I thought to myself
as redneck poster boy
started getting to me
at the beginning
of my manhood

Betraying confidence
I did not have
I just need to pee
I said a little louder

You can't go in there
the sign said
colored only
no whites allowed

I went in anyway
looked like every
gas station restroom
I had ever seen
before or since
and except for the sign
it was no different
sink, toilet, urinal

despite what the sign said
the fixtures were all white
and none colored

Mystified I took a leak
in off-white porcelain
taking hold of
Jewish circumcised self
Holocaust rhythms
lambasting my soul
thinking thoughts of
redneck euphoria
humming the chorus to
"If they could see me now"
I took a leak anyway
even though the sign
said colored only

I did not go up
in a puff of smoke
I did not come down with some
rare infectious disease
I did wash my hands
though no color rubbed
off onto my fingers

You can't go in there
the sign said
colored only
no whites allowed

I went in there
wondering what
the sign really meant
I came out of there
knowing I would always
go in there

Even though such signs
appear to be down
they are still up in such minds
but I will always go in there
I will always go in there

HOOPSTERS

It all started on the playground
shooting hoops with friends.

There were five Larry's
in our neighborhood,
and when one mama shouted Larry
all five commenced to running.

Then there was the morning
three of us awaited
the High School bus.

We played horse
a basketball game
of ghostlike pretensions
winner takes all
to the next morning contest.

We aimed potshots at the basket
without acclaim a
time passing ritual.

Suddenly!
Larry Mohlman shouted
at Larry Kempster:
"You're just like a Jew
you can only do one thing!"

Because he kept shooting lay-ups,
was not basketball worldly and wise,
did not diversify his shots
and kept driving persistence
to the backboard.

I looked on in disbelief
just as suddenly realizing why Molhman
always picked on me since age of six.
So with hook shot in hand,
set shot from perimeter,
jump shot from downtown
this Larry
meaning Jaffe
asked that Larry
meaning Mohlman
if I shot just like a Jew too.

He did not answer
turning red as his hair
as I proceeded to
take him to the cleaners
while all I could think
about were showers.

CATTLE CAR

Dedicated to theWarring Organization who resisted tyranny.

"In addition to the harm the warriors wanted to inflict on the enemy they wanted to show the world that in spite of their isolation the Jews resisted the Nazi murder machine. It was important to show that the Jews did not go like lambs to the slaughter. In Poland the history of this event was recorded as a rebellion act executed by the Gwardia Ludowa... Jewish warriors were not mentioned even once in spite of the fact that not even one Pole participated. The Germans also contributed to the historical distortion by never admitting in public to the Jewish rebellion."

I cannot see myself boarding a train to oblivion
a rail to nowhere going along with the herd for a ride

I cannot see myself despite my Jewishness
going into a cattle car under anyone's volition
let alone my own

I cannot see myself riding the rails of a cattle car
packed inside like human sardines
and someone else
holds the keys to my future

I cannot see myself climbing into the car
nor letting my family climb in this car
without a fight

I see disheveled disoriented Jews going
for a ride, one-way tickets clutched in
hands not made of fists...

—they travel to Auschwitz or Buchenwald

I wonder about the travel agent
that sold these tickets
and the tour guide from hell
that gave them the ride

I cannot see vacationing in Poland as a holiday
This was not Noah's ark it was Hitler's ark,
Nazi's ark
—They were not taking two of every species
they were taking six million of one

But I cannot see myself walking calmly
without a fight,
suffering the dishonor of mental dismemberment
slowly to holocaust away.

—Number tattoos are not rosebuds or nametags

—Some say you were not there
I say I was and am reborn yet again...

This was death camp
and I do not hear cries of joy,
only the sounds of vultures parading in goosesteps.

But the Nazis were very polite in their violence
their uniforms crisply cut bleeding the fingers
that clutched them.

camps so spotless and scrubbed
even the ovens were self-cleaning
I wonder who made them.
The Nazis so well spoken—
relocation they preached,
the ghetto is so dirty, scour your soul,
clean up your act—
take a shower in this stall without drains

They said it so politely—
Very few resisted and went willingly
going on one-way holiday, bags packed
with all perishables
Where were the men
Where were the women
as mankind and children were
merchandised and victimized?

They were just following orders
the Nazis were just following orders
the Jews were just following orders
today's Nazis are still following orders

I cannot see myself following orders
I will not follow orders.

HEY IT'S JUST A GAME

I'm rooting
for the home team
my team

I pledge
allegiance to
the flag
of the united
states of sports
statistics and
memorabilia

I'm rooting for my team
my home team
the New York Jews
or the NY Kikes as
they are fondly known

Yesterday some
native Hebrews
came running out
to protest the game

They claimed we
were stealing their
heritage and mocking
their name
just because
our mascot
runs around the
field in native rew garb

He has those
cute spit curls
on the side
of his head

and he wears one of
those yarmulke things
a beanie on his head
and a prayer shawl
It's supposed to be
authentic so I don't
know what their problem is

After all it's just a game
and we make sure
that when we are rooting
for the team that we
use all the proper
gestures in the stands
we have practiced
copying our shoulder
shrugs from
vaudeville acts
they show on the big screen

When the whole
crowd shouts OY
it is enough to raise
the hairs on the back
of your head

We chant shalom
when the team
is up to bat
and seem undefeatable

We even know how
to do that little dance
Jews are known to do
at weddings and such
We are very authentic

Hava Nagilla
is a great tune
we sing
and dance to it
in the stadium
thousands
of us together

When our rabbi mascot
goes into his prayer dance
in the bleachers
he looks so real
he looks so Jewish
you would never
know he is not
I think they use makeup
to get that effect
or maybe he wears one
of those life masks
molded off a real rabbi

All I know is that he
really knows how
to get the crowd going
with his prayers and stuff

I heard next year
they may get another
guy out there with him
who can sing
they call him
a cantor or something
I think because of
Eddie Cantor
a dead Jewish singer guy

I don't know what
these Hebrews are
complaining about
We are honoring them
and paying tribute

When our little Jews
run the base paths
we cheer them on
screaming l'chaim
another quaint
authentic Jewish saying

Personally,
I think it is
really picky
of them
to object

The mascot
and the team logo
look so authentic

REFLECTIONS ON MY UNCLE LOUIE ON A THURSDAY MORNING

My great uncle Louie is
long gone but never forgotten
living his life in relative thoughts
like rainbows for a cloudy day

Uncle Louie came from my
mother's side of the family tree
more like a grandfather
than uncle to me

He was grand in the tradition
of being great
handing people bootstraps
so they could lift themselves up
the mountains of life and out of
the valleys of their despair

He was a benevolent man
a businessman and business came first
except family came before that

He wore grey suits and
black knit button up shirts
strangely casual before his time
fondest memories
of him were our trips
to the neighborhood candy store
and sadly there are no more
candy stores where you
can drink a chocolate malted or
buy a PEZ dispenser
and no counterman soda jerk
to make you an egg cream
half built with nostalgia and foam

My great Uncle Louie holding
my 5-year-old fingers in his hand
as we took our weekly trek
footsteps caterwauling the pavement
to our candy store of chocolate dreams
and 10 cent toys made in paradise

Once when I was sad he found me
crying into the sidewalk
my tears making mud pies

Uncle Louie came
to my rescue
clasping his finger
with my tiny hand as
we proudly walked
to our candy store
chock full of fantasy

To make my smiles come alive
he bought me this tiny rocket
that exploded on impact
striking the sidewalk
like bombs away over Tokyo
like we used to say
but would not dream of now

You wound up and threw
this rocket way high in the air
and bam caps explode
in childish shrills

I walked with my Uncle Louie
smoking chesterfields by the dozen
I think he smoked cigarettes so
he would always have a reason
to go back to our candy store

where he bought them at less than
a quarter a pack and did not worry
about televised diseases catching
up with him

He liked going to the candy store
stocking up on Hershey's
Sno-Caps and Junior Mints
Clark Bars & Snickers
but no 3 Musketeers for him

He always had plenty
of Pep-O-Mint Lifesavers

He saved many a child's life
with his candy
not to mention
keeping an entire
fleet of dentists
in business

REFLECTIONS ON MY AUNT MARTHA ON A THURSDAY MORNING

There is this very nice
Jewish lady
what you might call the
grandmotherly type
certainly the prototype
matriarch ruling her roost
with the epitome of lioness pride

This extraordinary lady
my Great Aunt Martha
wife of my great Uncle Louie
for whom I have more
than just some affection

She is not only a woman
but also a lady
as in hey lady cause jerry Lewis
would certainly love her
as everyone in my family
very much does

This very nice Jewish lady
is not necessarily Jewish
in the religious sense
although she has a beautiful
mezuzah embellishing her door
proudly high on the jam

I bought it for her in a fit
of religious fervor on my part
and I don't know that she
kisses it every time she walks by
but I do get the feeling
it makes her feel
warm and safe all over

My Aunt Martha
is Jewish worthy
in the family tradition sense
She is Jewish to her roots
which are not dyed
retaining their original color
and unique flavoring

She is full of goose bump
feelings for everyone
she touches

She helped make a man
out of her nephew boy
never turning other cheeks
only the one to be kissed

I often got lost in her couch
one of those big old things
that when you sat in them
you disappeared for a week
or more

One time I thought they would
have to call the Mossad to
rescue me from cushions
turned Philistines

After she looked at me
she would turn to my mother
shrug her shoulders
saying oy at the same time
that Larry he is so melodramatic
My Aunt Martha makes potato latkes
like nobody's business
and her business is love

She would just eat you up
when you were little
now she is a grandma and greater
and you want to eat her up
like that plate of latkes
she displays for you every visit

You can feel the hard edges
crackle with the first crisp
bite and open you up to
a starchy euphoria
that literally has you
begging for more

Taking your plate
into the kitchen
to that ancient
broken-in frying pan
she's had for lifetimes
of Jewish Soul Food Cooking

You stand there
mouth open
eyes drooling
tongue doing
the funky chicken
to get another taste
watching the crackle and
sizzle of potato nirvana

I can never forget the
flavor of my Aunt Martha
or her latkes

REFLECTIONS ON MY COUSIN IRIS ON A THURSDAY MORNING

My cool cousin Iris is
something like 6 years
older than me

We were almost
born on the same day
her breaking out on the 30th
and me making
birthright bail on the 31st
of the month that goes in like a lion
and supposed to go out like a lamb
'cept we both be lions you know

Those 6 years were not a gap
more like a brief vacation
till we got to know each other again

My cool cousin Iris is the
progeny of my Great Uncle Louie
and my Great Aunt Martha
both of whom i am most fond

I remember her
walking me to school
our pudgy school children
fingers linked in destiny
My cousin Iris was
born wearing beatnik black
but she was not in mourning
beatniks only wear black
to mourn society
not their newborns
wearing widow's weeds

When I was little
and hardly charming
I wanted to be just like
my cool cousin Iris

She was finger-snapping hip
beat teen artist type idol
to my preteen years

When I was 12 having my first
kissing party full of post office
and spin the bottle
and Candy Cohen gave me a
Johnny Mathis album
but did not come to the party
cool cousin Iris was in the
Greenwich Village of my dreams

My cousin Iris was so cool
Greenwich Village artist cool
living on Jane Street where
the village began
and art had someplace to live
without a token existence

She drew life with charcoal
and sculpted from cold-faced stone
with her fingers chipping away
at the cocoon she was escaping

I never knew anyone like my cousin Iris
stuck back in that middle-class backyard
where I was trying to grow away

She was the butterfly
unwrapping herself
from mediocrity
the silken strands

of her past home
now being woven
into black turtleneck sweaters
she habitually wore
with nun-like precision
worshiping Eros
and other pretenders
to her throne

It took me 38 years to realize
she was my first crush

She was the first butterfly
to leave home
I wanted to follow her

She drank from coffee cups
I wanted to wrap my fingers around
She swam upstream in rivers
I wanted to bathe in
She talked to people
I longed to embrace
She grew up
I never did
still pushing my dreams in poetry
and wearing beat black

BLUE COLLAR FATHER

My father worked in
a factory when I was born
he was an artist that traded
his labor for a weekly paycheck
to raise a family
his art never appreciated

He was a factory kind of guy
working for his family's living
while his art was dying
my father's hands were
callused and raw
no longer those
of an artist

They wore the paint
of the factory
not the paint
from the palette
and though his hands
became pitted and hard
he could fix anything

People came from
all over the neighborhood
to feel his hands on their
toaster, washer or car

He could fix anything
anything but the thing he
wanted to fix the most
- me
Through my rebelliousness
and my crazies
I can see my father's
blue collar eyes

looking through me
trying to find me through
my own mirage and illusions

My father's blue collar hands
wanting to spank
the devil out of me
but holding back his tears
because he knew he
could not fix me

Strangely enough
his blue collar love
has now lasted
four lifetimes
four generations
his
mine
my daughters
and now my
our grandsons

PINSTRIPE SUITS

I grew up wanting to wear a pinstripe suit
No, not the kind that banker's wear.

I wanted to wear the pinstripes that adorned
my baseball heroes, those New York Yankees
legends of the long ball, running the outfield
that skirted my Bronx birthplace.

See, I was born in the shadow of Yankee stadium;
just down the street where Bronx hospital rocked
with muse in daily delivery— March 31st 1948.
I was born so bad I slapped that doc and pinched the nurse
No one touches my butt without permission

But, oh, I wanted to wear that uniform,
put spikes on my feet, run the infield, slide into home,
Grace the house that Ruth built, DiMaggio reigned
and Mantle owned.

They dressed in sports regalia, as if it were religion
they pursued and not homeruns, They wore
Holy Roller pinstripes; holy trinity of Ruth, DiMaggio
and Mantle crossed their bats and hoped to hit.

I longed to dress in locker rooms and hear my name
called on public address systems, look into the sun
and catch fly balls and pound my bat at the plate
making ready to be the next Sultan of Swat,
Yankee Clipper or the Mick.

I was born in the Bronx,
lived above a dry cleaning store—
I had to play catch with myself.

I grew up wanting to dress in pinstripes
and wear that Yankee suit
because I could never wear a tie without
feeling enslaved.

I wanted to roam centerfield
not a factory or an office.
And if I couldn't play baseball,
then I had to be a poet.

CONDOMS WITHOUT LOVE

You know they
give condoms out
to kids today
give them out in schools
as part of higher education

I started wondering about
these condoms
like what brand they use
and whether or not
the Trojan company
was cosponsoring the
event sort of like Nike does
on the playground

I could not imagine that
these condoms saw much love
you see it used to be tough
to get condoms
and it became some
kind of tribal ritual
that guys went through
so they could be all
grownup and a man
sort of like a bar mitzvah
only tougher

It used to be so
tough to buy a condom
and scary too
going into that dark
dreary drug store

and you had to find one
a drug store that is
that your parents never
went to nor anyone else
you knew for that matter
it certainly would not work
to be looking for Trojans
and have your aunt walk
in the door let alone your folks
or heaven forbid a girl
from your class or school

MILES SHOWED ME HIS TRUMPET

Miles Davis lived around the block from me
deep in the upper west side of Manhattan island.

He played like one man could be an island
living for his horn that paid his daily bread
living in this house made of gingerbread, on
West 77th Street while I lived on West 76th.

I would see him every now and again going
into that brownstone that his horn built.

— I got to meet miles

Walked round the block, walked round
the clock where Miles stood outside his
homestead just proud as peacock.

He told me how much he liked San Francisco women
because their bottoms were so round not flat
from riding subways all days, he said with smile.

Nudging me, guy hood joke "You know what I mean."

We went inside past the New York façade
into his musical domain —
headquarters for lonely horn players

The purity of Miles' trumpet leans into me
he sings it blue. My eyes tear uncontrollably.
He has touched melodies that riff with magic,
I escape ego with this horn. It is evolution of life
in notes counterpoint. My fingers feel broken,
wanting to make the same sounds with words
that staccato lip thing that merges horn with man.

— Miles showed me his trumpet
in this house of sugar coated dreams.
When I was a kid I dreamed of playing trumpet
but I wore braces on my teeth... they said I would
cut my lips to ribbons and bleed on my horn.

I looked up with tears and thought Miles,
Miles always bleeds on his horn

ARTIST

I have always
loved to watch
an artist work
whether
on canvas
piano
clay
or in a factory
at a sewing machine
or a saw where
work becomes art
on a basketball court
or a baseball field where
sport becomes art

I love to watch
the movements
of fingers doing
what they do best
or a voice that
captures passion
and the lust of life
the litany of a
head cocked just so
in the full
appreciation of themselves
and their work.

—So much there
yet no effort
as even the sweat glides
from their brow.

I admire these artists
and take delight not only
in their creations
but in their creating

I had the opportunity
to see another artist
with his fingers
at the keyboard

in virtuoso performance
interestingly enough
it was me.

—Tonight when I woke
in the middle of the night
I sat at my keyboard
and wailed.

Words went flying from
my fingers in song
my eyes crying salt
I had arrived for myself
and saw the expression
on my face
the rhapsody
of my fingers

I felt good
like Miles on the trumpet
Herbie at the piano
Picasso at the canvas
Dr. J. Soaring to the hoop
Mantle at the plate
Mays basket catching infinity
and my dad at his workbench.

—I felt like me

The words
like notes drifting
soaring
singing
lasering

and they knew
as I know
that I was born again
an artist

I'm A Poet Damn It

He said he was a poet
and came by
his right
to be sullen and moody
most righteously.
He said this with
with outrage
and indignation.

And I wondered
what kind of an excuse
Is that?
Was that?
Could I be moody
and call myself a poet
just like that
at a snap of fingers?

Which brings to mind
I could now
snap my fingers unforgiving.
I could walk down the street
snapping my fingers
and people from all over
would come up to me
and ask me
what I was doing?

I could just look at them
with this smile on my face
and say
I'm a poet damn it!

But that's not all
there is more to this story
I got run out of New York City
for being a poet.

I lived on 76th street
near Riverside Drive
My apartment was the size of a Twinkie
But it had a terrace
There were no real rooms

It was more like a closet
with a bath
and said terrace.

One night
not too late
I decided to perform poetry
from my terrace
overlooking the Henry Hudson River.

I would rain words down on society
every unassuming passerby
would be enabled
no empowered to hear my poetry.

I dressed in black
People looked up at me
and smiled
some would wave
some would say hello
some would laugh
some would curse at me.

The beautiful women
who lived
across the street

continued to parade naked
in front of the window.
I never knew if it was for my benefit
or their own.
There were three of them
all blonde.

I appreciated my view
Of river and beauty
and I appreciated that I could
poetize spontaneously
without combusting.
For a moment I felt
just like a poet
damn it!

And that moment seemed
to last a lifetime
Some would laugh
I hung on to that
terraced poetic perfection
with my last words.
Suddenly
sirens rifled may air
a huge searchlight
scanning the building
for outlaws and
chasing scofflaws.
The beam searched
relentlessly for words
left hanging
from the walls.

A blue-suited megaphone
shouted
up into the apartment hierarchy

YOU UP THERE!
They searched
for this disturber of the peace
they wanted him to come forward
and identify himself.

The women across the way
got dressed
saving my life,
alerting me
to the dangers lurking below

where New York's Finest
danced in criminal pursuit minuet
searching for my desperate tune.

I disguised myself in trench coat
slipped outside
without benefit of I. D.
I politely asked the head cop
What are you doing?
What's going on?
Was there a murder I asked?
He shook his head!
Was there a break-in I wondered
for there was massive manpower
now on west 76th street
four cop cars
with bubblegum machines blazing
stopped all traffic on the street
removing my audience.

The cop with megaphone was serene
going about his business with
Dirty Harry mentality.
He kept shouting for me

to stand down and surrender.
Only I was not there
I was standing next to him
devil may care and
not making his day.

I asked again
what's going on?
He replied with
Clint Eastwood finality
there's someone up there
talking to people
without permission!
And we're here to stop him
he is endangering the community
disturbing the peace!

You need this show of force
To detain him?
I inquired

The cop squawked
He is armed and dangerous!
He might be loaded
Scratched my head
Showed I was on his side
I whispered in his ear
He's a poet
Damn it!

UNPROTECTED POETRY

I had unprotected poetry last night
it was unexpected you know
spontaneous and we did not use anything
we just went at it to keep the mood.

It was incredible but not safe
and now I am worried
cause it can be infectious and dangerous
to say things without a condom.

It could be disastrous to speak without protection

A guy should not have unprotected poetry
he should take more responsibility than that
not just leave it up to the girl.

It was so irresponsible of me
to have unprotected poetry
to not even ask or consult
her about poetry control methods
she might be using or gulp not using.

What if she gets poetically pregnant
and wants to have my poem?

Or what if she has some kind
of poetically transmitted disease
you know PTD –
and we have to wait
and see what happens
taking regular poetry tests
to see if we've got it.

But wow
we actually did it last night –
We had poetry...
How many people
in this day and age
have pure unprotected poetry?
We should be thankful for that
after all it was good poetry
we both really enjoyed it!
We soared like angels
without wings
never coming down
just coming
poetically, that is.

But what a high
to hit that climax
and feel like you
will never be mortal again...

Now that you've had
unprotected poetry
who can protect you?
Now that you've had
unsafe poetry
and want to do it
again and again
and again...

Cause it don't feel
the same
with a poetic condom
blocks off the all feeling
and the flow.

And the words
the words
are stopped short
with safe protected poetry
and I will never
write that way again!

Jaffe has been writing since he was eight years old when he first learned he had captured the beauty and impact of words writing "Uncle Larry's Nature Column" for his camp newspaper. He has used a lot of ink since then. He still carries a small Moleskine notebook in his back pocket to capture those moments of inspiration. But after all those years of analog, he is thinking of switching to being completely digital. His new Samsung S4 is a gadget of creative wizardry and he can dictate or write into it with instant transcription.

Jaffe is an internationally known and an award winning writer, author and poet and founder of Poets Beyond Borders (a group dedicated to human rights and reform) and iSpeax his personal writing forum. Jaffe has been hosting and curating poetry readings for several years while also co-founding Poetix Poetry Magazine (a guide to Southern California Poetry). Additionally, Jaffe was a featured poet for Daimler/Chrysler's Spirit in the Words poetry program. Jaffe impacts audiences and readers with a rich emotional range, masterfully crafted, written from the heart and soul with clarity and understanding. Jaffe has read his work in such distinguished locations as the Japanese American Museum, the Hammer Museum, the Museum of Tolerance, the Jewish Museum and the Museum of Literature in Prague and the Dylan Thomas Centre in Wales.

Jaffe uses the aesthetic power of poetry to bring understanding to the world. He was the 2007 recipient of the Saint Hill Art Festival's Lifetime of Creativity Award, the first time given to a poet. He is the former poet in residence of the Autry Museum of Western Heritage. Jaffe spearheaded along with Rattapalax Publisher Ram Devineni the United Nations Dialogue among Civilizations through Poetry project which incorporated hundreds of readings in hundreds of cities globally using the aesthetic power of poetry to bring understanding to the world.

Writing is his life – he breathes in letters and breathes out words.

www.lgjaffe.com

www.Facebook.com/LarryJaffe

22931216R00030

Made in the USA
Charleston, SC
04 October 2013

7